don't read this book if you want to be spared

erin bryl

ISBN 979-8-9994841-0-9 (paperback)

dedicated to all the people, places, and things
that have come and gone along the way.

dedicated, also, to myself.
my selves? the label doesn't matter.
thank you, me.

Introduction

Author's Note

Hello. This book compiles much of my abstract, unrestricted poetry from the past five years and puts it in a single place with a relative direction. Maybe it even tells a story of sorts— it feels as though I've taken a thread and woven it through the pages, tying together some unintentional themes along the way.

If you know me in real life, you probably know that… well, actually, I'm not sure how I'm perceived. Apparently I come across as very closed off to some people and very open to others. I guess I live a paradox, in a way. A sharp contrast. (Thank the trauma for that one, I suppose.) So, if you don't know me as well as you'd like— meaning I haven't already spilled my entire inner mechanism to you— perhaps this is a good starting point. Most of my work is minimally edited; I shift it around as I go, and rarely do I touch it again afterwards. So some of it's not polished, which is the point, I think.

The way these poems are organized is largely chronological in the dates that they were first written. I collected them over time, then forgot about them, then remembered once I picked up writing again. Thankfully I saved the oldest ones from being erased before I graduated high school, although I'm sure a few did unfortunately get lost forever. That's okay. Most of them were salvaged.

When thinking about a format for this book, I initially wanted to use a handwritten font and illustrate each page to imitate how my personal journals feel. However, it occurred to me that that would be like giving you, the audience, answers to the questions you didn't even know to ask yet. So I settled on a more minimal layout. You're going to come to your own conclusions about my words regardless of how I present them, and why would I hinder your thoughts in favor of centering mine? They're already the focal point of my work.

If by the end you really are curious, you're more than welcome to ask me what my ideas mean— but I want you to trust your imagination, too. I'm certain that if you do that, you will get to where I'm standing, and if not, that you will find yourself exactly where you're supposed to be at the time of reading.

-Erin

A Warning

To all the people who wouldn't understand.
Maybe they would, and I've assigned them a label;
It seems more likely that they'd get some of it,
and not other parts, but not show any of that.
Expressing your thoughts is not quite palatable.

I don't know what you know—
about yourself, about others, about anything at all—
if you don't let me know.
And I'm tired of dragging my feet,
preparing to ask but never doing it.
Or dragging my feet because
I've asked and gotten answers,
but never have they lasted.
Those exchanges, I mean. They are not continual.
They stop at the end of the gathering
and don't get picked up or looked at again
unless I drag my feet and do it myself.

Vulnerability is weak, or so it is perceived that way,
when really it takes a certain mixture
of bravery, discontentment, and lost status
to step out of the shadows that hide a face.
This goes for those of us who have been degraded
and molded against ourselves, at least.
As for the children presently unfazed,
standing strong with their toes in the dirt,
I just hope we nourish their will to return
to their inner homes time and time again.
They will not remain unscathed—
None of us ever were, nor ever will be—
But that does not mean they must
jump off the highest ledge like so many
who came before them, like so many around them,
and spend most of their lives in the pit
simply because we told them they should.
That is unnecessary.

So lend me a hand, just as I extend
a hand to you (often time and time again);
And let us see ourselves a way out of this together.

And now, if you're still here:
What you're supposedly looking for.

Contents

2021–2022

A spring depression
(the collection)

dreams

floating
i'm floating
high up, well above
the clouds

i look down and
see
the lights
getting dimmer
quivering
in the cold

wind rushes around me but
i stay perfectly still
paralyzed, but not in fear
just understanding

i see it now
how the rustling of leaves
are gone, and
just the cityline
is visible
it’s all that's left for me

maybe there's people down there,
i don't know
i shouldn't worry much about it
because they're not here for me

they're here for each other,
while i float
still, motionless
and
all alone

ruined

falling through a pre-constructed reality
clouds open up under my weight
watch me as i plummet down
i guess this is my fate

words, names, places fall upwards
useless in the sky
everything i've ever loved
i guess this means goodbye

desperate screams, frantic cries
i shudder in my sleep
wind chills me to the bone

or was it simply the absence
of my own name
up there?

ouch

the ground's impact shocks my spine
yet no blood comes out
surprising, didn't think i was a shell
guess we can't trust ourselves then

fractured, bruises sting and wince
twinge of loathe and shame
lying on polished concrete
i don't think i'll be the same

voices come and linger
whistle through their teeth
poke me, kick me, throw some rocks
why don't ya? i sure don't mind

point and holler if you want
maybe it'll do some good
while i sit here, dazed and paralyzed
but hearing each word
clearer than it's ever been before

so crystal it hurts

my nature

hopefully some flowers fester
eat up the rest of my life
make a new growth over my struggling body
put it to rest
y'know?

even they'll struggle to make it all better

The uncertainty takes hold

If I Could Pause Time

If I could pause time
I'd do it
It would stay that way
For a while

If the world were to slow,
I'm sure I'd spend my day
just chasing my breath
cuz it's floating away

i'd catch it in a
little jar, maybe
and carry it home
in my pocket

then empty it out
on the tabletop
and shove it back
into my body

No, not shove,
i'd inhale it gently
i've been rough enough
for us both

i'd cherish it, hold it,
sit quiet in a time
where the burning would cool
that i've loathed

where the clocks would stop ticking
the thorns would stop pricking
the space got a chance to
freeze over

the wind wouldn't claw
i wouldn't withdraw
then maybe i'd get to feel closer

The breath rattles and shakes
Not in rage, but in fear
As the timekeeper yanks
It away

He tells me "tsk, tsk",
Unpauses the clock,
And stands, watching
My smile
            slowly
                    fade

oh…

oh
i guess
i guess i’m not
i guess i’m not wanted here
  guess i’m not wanted here
  guess i’m not wanted
              i’m not wanted
                    not wanted
              i’m not
              i’m not   here
                    no

movement

The clock is moving forward
but time is moving back
and I'm not moving at all

them

How am i supposed to help a bag of sand?
Every time i heave upwards gravity pulls it back down
It makes no effort to move at all

But as soon as i start swaying it pushes down into the earth,
Popping right back up by my side
To sway all by itself and tell me i was wrong

Well, i'm sorry about that, i guess
I really am

Next time i try to help a bag of sand,
I think i'll just sit here and wait

Circling the Drain

Maybe if I hadn't
Maybe if I hadn't
Maybe if I hadn't
Maybe I shouldn't have
I'm sorry, I didn't know it went wrong
I thought I had done good

I should've known
I should've known
I should've known
What should I have known?
Probably something important
Has my face made you upset again?
I'm sorry

I'm sorry
I'm sorry
I'm sorry
I'm sorry
I'm sorry
I'm so sorry
My feelings must be wrong
Wrong
Wrong
Wrong
I remember wrong
I must be in the wrong

You're not anything other than fine
We're fine, we're good
They know
No, I said we're fine
We're fine
We're fine

Yeah, I'm okay! Sorry about that.

Distance

Stuck in a bubble
A squishy one
Squashed between time and space

Brain's in a bubble
Not quite rubble
But thick and squelching all the same

Am I here or am I gone?
Am I floating, prolonged?
I can't feel anything but my face

I want to go home
And crash into bed
Sink deeper, deep through the frame

This is a choice

letting go doesn't have to be as hard as it should be
sure, standing over a cliff's edge
holding nothing but a rope is terrifying
but really, where else do you have to go?

i, personally, want to stand here forever
watching my shoes' creases get deeper
and my jacket shrink
y'know, since i sure as hell haven't grown
while standing here

by this point, i think i'd rather be pushed over the ledge
than have to jump by myself
but there's no one around that would be willing
or i'd even trust to let me fall

letting go shouldn't be as hard as it is
only when you lose everything do you realize how little
you've truly lost
but i know i haven't learned that yet

guess i'll just… stand here
trying to convince myself
that maybe i'll be…
maybe?
maybe i'll be okay

A brief period of hope

Nurture

When even my heart beats faster
than my mind wants to go,
Does that mean i should follow it?
I don't think it does

I think it's my body's way of showing me
How capable it is of love
That is undirected

And that i should take the chance
To bring my love
Somewhere it's needed

That's what makes it a home,
A place that wants me
Protects me

Shares my joy, my triumph, and my loss
That isn't really loss,
Just learning

When even my heart beats faster
than my mind wants to go,
I'll know that means it loves me
Vowing to keep me warm and bright
Despite unforeseeable cold

Sinkhole

What happens if I take
the rose colored glasses off?
Will life still look the same?
I sure hope it's not as dreary
As the misery-seekers make it sound

If I take them off, maybe
it'll sigh but also settle
Into the ground that
Was meant to hold it

Maybe it'll fall down into dark
But this time, I think I'll get to
Walk around the opening,
Inspect it with utmost curiosity
Dangle my legs over the side
Knowing it would catch me
And lift me back up again

And the hole wouldn't grow bigger
This time around—
I think it would stay, breathing,
Relaxing into the hazard signs I built
The caution tape would rip a little
But we both know that's okay

Too Much

You ever wonder if you're too much?
But if you stopped moving
The world would stop spinning

Everyone else is walking while you run
Stepping while you stomp
In puddles, opening your mouth
To catch the rain

You jump and the ground shakes
And the people rattle, too
It puzzles them,
But nicely, I'd say
I mean, I hope it's nice

I hope they get confused by me,
And the funny way I walk,
And the funny little way I talk,
Like a tide of water rushing
That then stops, I hope

That maybe I get them
To see the sunshine, sometimes,
That they know it's alright
To walk through the snow if you feel like it
That the carousel can keep going

Even if it's time to get off
Because who says the park
Must shut down? It's my park,
After all— I make these rules

And the words that ramble by themselves—
they take up my mind's space—
They're allowed to spill out
As freely as they please,
So long as you don't mind it

So keep moving,
I say, keep flying;
For if you slammed the brakes
Life might halt screeching

Go lightly and take it slow
All you want, but please,
Don't stop laughing
And don't stop loving
The way you so love to do

And one day, you might notice
That the people may mind,
But the world loves you right back;
That you've planted a flower
For another child to pick.

at long last

She likes the sky when it pours
And the people she adores
All like to hear her living,
breathing, moving metaphors

She speaks out through her similes
She tiptoes on the sand
She kneels down in the water
And she runs it through her hands

She hums in hyperboles,
She skips across the walk
And if you wish her any good
Then by God, you'll hear her talk

She converses through her whistles
(She doesn't know how to whistle)
And she can't exactly say it
But she does feel bad just a little

She talks to inanimate objects
And tells them they look nice
She finds the risks that most have taken
And doesn't roll the dice

She writes down all her memories
And records all her dreams—
The real ones, when she's wide awake,
Because of how much they mean

She likes to just be happy
But sometimes she'll still freeze
She'll eternally be thankful
For her complex analogies

Often her words must come through
The form of a little box
It's neatly wrapped, though—
She tried her best
And she's glad you think it's enough

She feels she's living upside down
But she doesn't really see it,
Since most of the time there's someone there
Who comes and hangs out on the ceiling

The one thing that she fears the most
Is being all alone,
But lately she's noticed a garden of flowers
Surround her as they grow

She likes to feel accepted
And she hopes you know for sure
That your presence is the perfect place
To sing her metaphors

2023

(The Gap Year)

Rebuilding in September

You can see how the tiredness
presents in my eyes.
How castle's supports crumbled,
eroded by a tide
of tears soon dried.
You can feel the heavy sighs—
Gusts of bound-to-fail pride,
as the tensions subside,
leave a tower in shambles
and a defeated girl behind.

Some structure still abides
by the call of the times;
Though disheveled and on sand,
lights glow fairly inside.
But all it has stood through
and its current respite
does not soften past blows
of a generous might.

Echoed winds carry cries
though transcendence of time
which beat against the windows
with the memory of fight;
Tooth, nail, and blood
scattered, trailing the sky—
The faintest reminder:
that ease, too, can pass you by.

I bode you this caution,
for a part of me lies
clinging earnest to the fate
of a life left behind.

The downfall of a spirit
who'd been trapped and too wise
left a desolate abode
through begrudged compromise.

And thus, much of home is wounded
from the battle for a life,
which stands worthy of redemption
from the horrors of such night.
Miraculous, it seems,
for this haven to survive,
intact on moving ground through
storm's intent to undermine.

As a passing traveler told me
in most recent of times,
"Birds are singing, are they not?
So have faith in their chimes."
The land is not barren—
Sun and creatures both rise,
breathing life into the ruin
that you seem to chastise."

It holds space in my heart
to know someone wise as I;
Even moreso, perhaps,
as I cannot deny

There was something peculiar
about the glint in his eye,
and his "This doesn't scare me"
turned the burden quite light.

My mind wandered with him—
I do apologize.
A free spirit, he was,
and sometimes I might try

To let go of worry
and imitate his stride,
listen close to the nature
that stays at my side.

Protection surrounds us;
I must drop my guise,
fall to earth that will catch me
while part of me dies.
Soft grass holds my sorrows,
my grief, and my cries;
my aches, and my trembles
that almost remind

How destruction is imminent;
Still, I've realized
that the seasons rebuild
in a strengthened reprise.

I hold to my fear,
though its ego is wry,
slowly testing these waters
one dip at a time.

Please don't judge my hesitance;
I've walked without guide
for miles upon miles,
no affirmation in sight.

Don't heed my old warning—
I now would advise
to observe your own village,
and cut off some ties
that tether your being
to unending tides;
Don't pin your very worth
to what smoldering implies.

The land isn't leveled,
and the sea doesn't rise
to wash away ignition
of foreseeable fire.

I hope you may notice
how the tears in my eyes
hold exhaustion so strong
that I fear I'll capsize.
I hope, still, you recognize
how some of my sighs
convey not only weight,
but relief that coincides.

The house may have shifted
and fallen to time,
soon followed by hopes
treading close to thin lines.
But at last, the quakes ceased,
giving way to revise.

The earth will not leave
this disheartened girl behind.

2024–2025

A cacophony of chaos

Newly Escaped

Push all the air out of my lungs and
wonder why my chest stops moving,
choking out whispered tragedies.

Is it worth it to keep trying?
Do I have any choice?

Slice me at the knees and
ask if it hurts to run
when you see me stumble.

If I tell you no, you'll believe me.
You always do.

Hold the flowers at the funeral I won't have and
let it not cross your mind how many times
I must've collapsed before this.

Don't feel my palms.
They're rubbed raw.

When the rain falls, and it pours, and
the wind howls and blows it sideways,
look out the window and
appreciate its terrifying beauty.

The water will cascade out the downspouts.
Be grateful it's not trapped in the gutters.

When the ground opens up and
attempts to swallow you whole,
look up at the town around you and
say a prayer for what you'll lose.

The sinkhole may hold some sympathy.
Have some trust in the nature you stand on.

Glass

The glass shattered, and I prick myself
on the jagged edges on purpose,
willing them to be smooth.
There's slivers in my fingers.
I'm used to that.

I know I'm meant to pick up some pieces
and kick others aside like everyone
who came before me;
Hopefully I can take a part of myself
and kick it to the side too.
Maybe that's what will fix this.

Balancing

I can't walk straight after I've spun myself dizzy.
Do you know how uncomfortable that is to do?
You don't even know if you're doing it right.

Or when you step off the ride
and your friends immediately take off running,
while you're still getting used to feeling
the ground under your feet again.
Just give me a minute or two.

Possibility of Blood

Have you ever had a nosebleed,
And tilted your head back to get it to stop,
Only realizing your mistake
Once blood drained into your throat?
I'm choking on my words.

Spit it up, don't swallow.
I do this in theory.
Literally, I spit.
Metaphorically, I swallow.
The sink is stained vaguely red.

The bleed comes to distract me
As my mind rushes for tissues.
Sometimes, when there are none,
I hold my breath to keep it in.
It stays suspended.

Egoic

Like the daffodils after moderate rain,
Or the faucet running straight at the drain,
Water down my thoughts ‘til they’ve flattened;
And maybe then they will be palatable,
Not bitter or sour like inedible plants.

Wash my face with the flowing spout,
Freeing me through uncensored doubt.
Merely a mirage, I conclude,
While webs woven by spiders
Cloud the corners of my vision.

I can push away this nagging
With a funny sort of bragging-
Look how easy it is for me.
I’m right as a puddle being
Stepped in and splashed.

Muddled thoughts in a rocked boat

when i don't have the words,
would you still want me?
when i don't have words,
do you still know?

Oh, how loud a soul
And how quiet a tremor
A teeter-totter paradox

If my insides spill to the outsides, then…
then… then, well…
I'm at a loss.

Purify me
Cleanse my soul

the prettiest art comes
from the worst times

give me some of your life energy
and I will be sure to extend it tenfold
in all directions

put down your vices and rest in the stillness of nothing.
comfort in the absence of any real chaos. the towers can
fall later. for now, there is breath.

Lost once again

On Recognition

Am I supposed to expect
That you will understand me,
Or am I meant to hold the superstition
That you are glossy-eyed?
Different people tell me different things,
And at first few glances I cannot determine
Whether they are living with their vision
Behind moving water.
Even worse,
Those people then go on to believe
Their perception is clear
With no convincing them otherwise.

Perhaps I'm objectifying this,
Capturing it at an angle
That cannot possibly hold
The nuance it deserves.
To that I say fair enough—
I know in myself
I avoid exploration of said nuances,
Fearing the overwhelming vastness
Of the universe of possibilities that
No mortal could ever begin to fathom.
It is simply too much.

Dysfunctional Strides

Why are the people always running?
What for? Where to?
What are they chasing or escaping?
Are they just running to run?
Surely there must be more than that.
Surely, if they were to slow their gait,
Slower, slower, slower—
Sprint, to run, to jog, to walk, to stroll,
to dawdle, to drag, to stop—
Stop, to pause, to breathe, to crouch,
to sit, maybe even to lay—
Sit, to lay, to sigh, to look,
to feel, to see, to realize…

Well, maybe they would observe,
For once in their specified lifetime,
The earth that flutters and the trees that shake
And the grass that ruffles and the breeze that breaks
And the conscience inside them yelling,
"I'm a being! I'm a being!".
Perhaps it even cries, wails, bellows,
Kicks, screams, lashes out in tides of thunder,
Of storm, of winds, of whirling noise, of chaos
that is thought to only be found in nature.
Can it be said, then, that you are nature?
How would you ever learn this
if you were to not stop running?

People race past me, involved in a hunt—
Are they the chaser or the chased?
Likely neither, but it also isn't
the quest they think it is,
as that is not accurate;
But I am not like them.
I have never been affiliated,
despite the attempts to grab me
and pull me up from the ground
as they move on by.
"Why aren't you running?",
they hardly have time to say,
and the shaping of their question
is exactly my answer.
I will not flee my own scene
that will follow me regardless
of my strenuous efforts,
giving me not a moment of peace
and for no reason at all.

I will choose to sit and to listen,
and, when I offer, the little being
so capable of being pushed away
shows its magnitude of the role
it plays in my own reality.
You cannot shake off a creature
that has a permanent hold on you.
Try building it a nice home
and perhaps you'll see it
not to be bothersome in the slightest;
In fact, it will treat you much like a friend
who you will find yourself belonging to
for a very long time.
Your purposes will undoubtedly align
if you let them.

in hindsight

did you smell the desperation?
could you feel how it reeked, perhaps lingered?

there's a lot of things I wish I could say to you.

self-excavation

rip, claw my way out of the ground.
finally— finally— i can touch the air.
muggy and warm, it is better than stale nothingness,
and soon it will be breezy and cooled;
a shorter length of time than it took
to successfully dig upwards
when you weren't sure
which way was up.

A way forward (?)

spring cleaning

the closet door has opened
the things are sprawled on the floor
i stand there, looking at them
it's not as much as i figured it'd be

maybe it's more dense than it appears?
i'm not sure yet
maybe that's not all of it
maybe there is a house full of endless stuff
and this is just the coat closet
i'm not certain yet

but this, this feels manageable
i have not been flooded with
a pile of nightmares as i had anticipated
the beast is really quite small
there just happens to be many of them
running around, knocking things over
and acting like children
you know: exclaiming, exploring,
loving, fearing, despairing
over things so small and so large
at the same time
i suppose we parallel one another

well, i guess i'd better get
to doing some sort of work
or do i need to, yet?
an inkling tells me strongly
that i can move as slowly as i please
dawdle, in fact, with the intention
of feeling every inch of the pile
getting to know the mess
like the back of my hand,
which i also do not know yet

make like the beast children,
i tell myself,
and leave a signature
telling of your presence
in the place, at the time,
contributing to the chaos
it's like their tidal wave pool
is only three feet deep,
but the waves are mighty

coming from adoration

i had not loved before.
not after the first time.

love is a forbidden word in my mind, for i had
misinterpreted it, with my desperation brushed aside.
love is not the cries, screams, bellows stricken
with fear. i'm quite certain i know this for sure.
what i do not know is how to put a label on love.
so i shall wander with it instead.

love is in the rhythmic calm of the sea.
love is in the roots infiltrating the ground,
giving liveliness to the earth underneath us.
love is the liveliness. not the intensity,
but the certainty of the inner workings,
the mechanisms we cannot separate from.
no, not mechanisms. machinery does not last.
nature does. automation is as cyclical in its death
as our existence is in its own surefire being.

water (my perspective)

grief is like a river
it all depends on what the noise means for you

can you sink or would you swim?
do you believe so?
or are you happy not knowing?

ix (the hermit)

and here we are again.
we've come back around for the fifth time,
the ups and downs of a lonely walk
through a forest of everchanging paths.
the disappearance of friends as you
enter the leaves, the brush,
and come out the other side more
enlightened than you were before.
i'd say it's an increase in perceptual ability.
the grass is not greener upon emergence,
but the earth sure is more detailed.

in underlying anticipation we fear stagnancy.
mud that never moves. you can taste it.
we are averse to wallowing in this sensation.
even thinking it makes my skin crawl.
would you prefer this, or the roundabout
of swimming in invisible riptides?
perhaps neither is better than the other,
as they go hand in hand.

we do anything to gain control in this regard,
when really, what have you gained?
narratives don't shift unless you step off the trail
and let them follow you.
eventually they would catch up and
walk by your side, ready to collaborate,
but we don't tend to wait that long.
we are impatient—
no, it is more so that we are scared.

i am weary of seeing cloaks.
we hold the belief that they are
the only thing keeping us safe,
and so we huddle in them and
shut out the call of the birds.
ironic, isn't it, how we've
deemed the sounds of nature,
particularly of divinity, to be our downfall.

. . .

what am i so afraid of?

and here we are again.
we've come back around for the sixth time,
working through a rough patch
we did not know was there.

Final Note

Hello once more. I'm not exactly certain what I should put here, but surely some words belong in this space, so adding words is what I will do.

This book feels like it came out of thin air, when, really, it's been slowly constructed over the course of my later adolescence and rapidly assembled right at the end. Truthfully, it's been hard to read back, even for editing purposes. Piecing together my most recent life phases all at once like that is a lot. But hopefully it helps you to get an idea of where I've been and potentially where I'm going next.

I think my intention behind this compilation is to put myself out into the world more than I ever have. Not in a small way, or a polished way, or even in a careless way— all of which are ways that I have expressed myself before. No; This is a bigger, more open way. Because I want to be open, as open as I was before I was shoved into a box and then too afraid (or smart) to leave. Because I have an opportunity to not be trapped in my own mind anymore. I'm learning there is nothing stopping me from doing what I want except my own self. Honestly, there never was, besides the consequences of other people's reactions. And I can now afford more than before not to center my decisions around that.

If you're here reading this, and you feel stuck in your life, I hope you got something out of my words. That something made you think, or gave you a little perspective, a little leverage somewhere. I like opening pathways for people like that. Maybe it'll inspire you to make your own thing and share it, even if it's just to a couple of people. I hope so. The world needs authentic exchanges. It's what makes life fun.

This may have turned into more of a ramble than a cohesive ending, but that's okay. All I said was that I would put words here, and for all intents and purposes I succeeded, so that's fine by me. I guess what I want to leave off saying is this:

Here's to a brighter future for us all, because for the first time I do believe we have the power to create one.

-Erin

www.ingramcontent.com/pod-product-compliance
Lightning Source LLC
LaVergne TN
LVHW011049110826
845149LV00015B/3420

* 9 7 9 8 9 9 9 4 8 4 1 0 9 *